Smart Real Estate Investing

Discover Lucrative Properties Stress-Free for High Returns

NELLA BYRAN

Contents

Opening

In the dynamic realm of real estate, the quest for lucrative investments often intertwines with the labyrinth of complexity and stress. For those seeking to navigate this landscape with finesse and emerge victorious, "Smart Real Estate Investing: Discover Lucrative Properties Stress-Free for High Returns" serves as a guiding light, illuminating a path that transforms the intricate world of real estate into a realm of opportunity and financial prosperity.

This book is a compass for investors—both seasoned and aspiring—who harbor the desire to harness the wealth-generating potential inherent in real estate. In the sections that follow, we embark on a journey that transcends the traditional barriers of complexity and analysis paralysis, inviting readers to explore a universe of possibilities where stress is replaced by strategic wisdom and high returns become the norm rather than the exception.

The journey begins with a comprehensive exploration of the fundamentals that underpin smart real estate investing. This initial immersion into the fundamentals serves as a catalyst for the transformative journey that follows and as we progress through the sections, a strategic roadmap unfolds, leading investors through the nuanced terrain of property identification and analysis.

The importance of location in real estate is a timeless adage, and one of the Sections of this book delves into this critical factor with precision.

The integration of technology in real estate analysis is explored and we unveil the power of data analytics.

Each section is a building block, contributing to a comprehensive framework that empowers readers to make calculated decisions and navigate the complexities of real estate transactions with confidence.

This book is not merely a theoretical guide; it is a practical manual enriched with negotiation tactics, case studies, and a deep dive into the psychology of successful real estate investment. It bridges the gap between theory and practice, ensuring that readers are not only well-informed but also adept at translating knowledge into tangible results.

In "Smart Real Estate Investing," the intention is not merely to impart knowledge but to foster a mindset—a mindset that embraces opportunity, values strategic wisdom, and navigates challenges with resilience. As readers embark on this journey, they will discover that the pursuit of lucrative properties need not be a stress-laden endeavor; instead, it can be a transformative expedition toward financial prosperity and real estate mastery. Welcome to the world of smart investing, where stress gives way to strategy, and high returns become a tangible reality.

Section 1: Fundamentals of Smart Investing

The Fundamentals of Smart Investing in Real Estate

Smart investing in real estate is an art that extends beyond mere property acquisition; it encompasses a comprehensive understanding of the underlying principles that drive success in this dynamic market. The Fundamentals of Smart Investing in Real Estate, serves as a crucial primer, laying the groundwork for readers to navigate the intricate world of real estate with confidence and strategic insight.

At the core of smart investing lies a profound understanding of the unique characteristics of real estate as an asset class. Real estate, unlike stocks or bonds, is tangible and has the potential for both appreciation and income generation. The section begins by unraveling these fundamentals, emphasizing the enduring nature of real estate as a cornerstone of wealth creation. By grasping the intrinsic value of property, investors are equipped with the foundational knowledge necessary to make informed decisions.

One of the fundamental pillars of smart real estate investing is the strategic identification of emerging trends in the property market. Understanding the dynamics that drive market shifts is essential for staying ahead of the curve. Investors learn to discern patterns, anticipate changes, and position themselves to capitalize on emerging opportunities. The ability to identify trends enables investors to adapt their strategies to evolving market conditions, ensuring that their portfolios remain resilient and responsive.

Investors are guided in uncovering hidden gems by evaluating factors such as proximity to amenities, neighborhood growth potential, and overall market demand. Mastering this aspect ensures that investors are not just buying properties but strategically positioning themselves in areas poised for long-term success.

The power of data analytics emerges as another fundamental in the arsenal of smart real estate investors. Section 1 delves into the transformative role of data in decision-making. Analyzing market trends, demographic data, and economic indicators becomes a strategic imperative. Investors learn how to leverage technology and data tools to gain a competitive edge, transforming what may seem like complex analysis into actionable insights.

Furthermore, the section addresses the cyclical nature of real estate markets. Navigating these cycles intelligently is fundamental to maximizing returns. Understanding when to enter the market, when to hold, and when to exit can significantly impact an investor's success. This cyclical awareness is coupled with a nuanced discussion on the art of timing—an integral element in the pursuit of high returns.

In essence, this Section serves as a comprehensive guide to the fundamentals that constitute smart investing in real estate. From recognizing the enduring value of real estate as an asset class to mastering the intricacies of location, data analytics, and market cycles, readers are equipped with the knowledge necessary to embark on a journey of strategic and stress-free real estate investing. It lays the groundwork for the subsequent sections, where these fundamentals are further refined and applied in the pursuit of lucrative properties and high returns.

Identifying Emerging Trends in the Property Market

In the ever-evolving landscape of real estate, the ability to identify and capitalize on emerging trends is a hallmark of savvy investors. At its essence, identifying emerging trends involves a keen awareness of the factors that shape the property market's trajectory. This section begins by emphasizing the importance of staying informed about macroeconomic trends that influence real estate. Economic indicators, interest rates, and demographic shifts are among the key drivers that can foretell the direction of the market. Understanding these factors enables investors to align their strategies with broader economic forces, positioning themselves for success.

Demographic trends play a pivotal role in shaping the demand for different types of properties. As populations grow, age, and change in composition, so do their housing needs. Section 2 delves into the intricacies of demographic analysis, helping investors decipher patterns related to population growth, migration, and lifestyle preferences. By discerning these demographic shifts, investors can anticipate the demand for specific property types, ensuring their investments align with evolving market preferences.

Technological advancements represent another influential force in the property market. The section explores how innovations in technology can create new opportunities and reshape the real estate landscape. The rise of smart home technology, virtual property tours, and block chain applications in real estate transactions are among the trends covered. Investors who embrace these technological shifts gain a competitive edge, enhancing their ability to adapt to changing consumer expectations and market dynamics.

Societal and cultural shifts are integral components of emerging trends in the property market. Section 2 encourages readers to consider how changing lifestyles, preferences, and cultural norms impact real estate. The rise of remote work, for instance, has led to a surge in demand for homes with dedicated office spaces, altering the dynamics of property markets in suburban and rural areas. Understanding these shifts enables investors to anticipate future demands and tailor their investments accordingly.

Environmental and sustainability trends are gaining prominence in the property market. This section discusses how eco-friendly and sustainable features are becoming key considerations for both residential and commercial properties. Investors who align their portfolios with the growing emphasis on sustainability not only contribute to environmental goals but also position themselves favorably in a market increasingly attuned to eco-conscious practices.

Global economic factors are explored as well, as the interconnected nature of the world economy influences property markets across borders. The section guides readers in understanding how international economic trends, trade dynamics, and geopolitical events can have ripple effects on local property markets. A holistic view that considers both local and global factors empowers investors to make more informed and resilient decisions.

In summary, "Identifying Emerging Trends in the Property Market" goes beyond a mere snapshot of current conditions; it equips readers with the tools to anticipate, adapt, and capitalize on the forces that will shape the future of real estate. By mastering the art of trend identification, investors position themselves not as passive participants but as proactive navigators of the evolving property market, ensuring their portfolios are positioned to thrive in the face of change.

Location, Location, Location: Finding the Hidden Gems

The age-old adage in real estate, "location, location, location," resonates profoundly in this Section as we embark on a detailed exploration of the significance of geography in real estate investment. Titled "Location, Location, Location: Finding the Hidden Gems," this section serves as a pivotal guide for investors seeking not just properties, but strategic positions within the real estate landscape.

At the core of this section lies the recognition that the value and potential appreciation of a property are intricately tied to its geographical location. It begins by elucidating the multifaceted aspects that define a prime location, extending beyond proximity to basic amenities. Readers are encouraged to delve into the micro and macro characteristics of a locale, unlocking the potential of hidden gems that might not be immediately apparent.

The section delves into the art of recognizing emerging neighborhoods poised for growth. Investors learn to identify early indicators such as infrastructure development, urban revitalization projects, and the influx of businesses and cultural amenities. By understanding the dynamics of neighborhood evolution, readers gain the foresight needed to position themselves in areas on the brink of transformation.

Accessibility, both current and future, becomes a key consideration in the quest for hidden gems. The section explores how transportation infrastructure, such as highways, public transit, and airports, can impact property values. Moreover, it delves into the evolving trends of remote work and the gig economy, emphasizing the importance of flexible commuting options and proximity to co-working spaces in contemporary property evaluation.

Demographic analysis is interwoven into the fabric of location-based considerations. The section guides investors in understanding the target demographic for their properties, recognizing that different locations attract distinct resident profiles. Whether it's young professionals seeking vibrant urban settings or families desiring suburban tranquility, aligning the property's location with the preferences of the target demographic enhances its appeal and potential for appreciation.

Beyond tangible factors, the section delves into the subjective yet influential aspects of neighborhood ambiance and community character. The "feel" of a location—its culture, safety, and community engagement—can significantly impact property values. Investors are encouraged to conduct thorough research and even engage with local communities to gauge these intangible yet vital elements that contribute to the overall desirability of a location.

The concept of hidden gems extends beyond well-known cities to include overlooked or emerging markets. The Section introduces readers to the notion that lucrative opportunities may not always be found in the most apparent locales. Exploring secondary or tertiary markets can unveil hidden gems with untapped potential, offering investors the advantage of entering markets before they become mainstream.

Strategic foresight is emphasized throughout the section, urging investors to think not just about the current state of a location but its future trajectory. By adopting a forward-thinking mindset, investors position themselves to benefit from the compounding effects of long-term appreciation and demand, transforming their properties into enduring assets.

In essence, "Location, Location, Location: Finding the Hidden Gems" transcends the cliché, providing a nuanced exploration of the factors that make a location truly exceptional. It is an invitation to see beyond the surface and recognize the hidden potential that lies within specific geographic contexts. As readers navigate this section, they gain a comprehensive understanding of the art of location selection—a skill that elevates real estate investing from mere transactions to strategic positioning for sustained success.

Unveiling the Power of Data Analytics in Real Estate

In the digital age, the fusion of real estate and artificial intelligence (AI) is transforming the landscape of property investment. Section 4, titled "Unveiling the Power of Data Analytics in Real Estate," explores the profound impact of AI and data analytics on the way investors analyze, predict, and strategize within the real estate market.

Data analytics utilizes algorithms and computational models to process vast amounts of information, unveiling patterns and insights that might elude traditional analysis methods. In the context of real estate, AI-driven data analytics becomes a powerful tool for investors seeking a competitive edge. One of the primary contributions of AI to real estate lies in its ability to process and interpret large datasets, offering investors a deeper understanding of market trends and dynamics.

Predictive analytics is a key facet of data-driven decision-making in real estate. AI algorithms can analyze historical property data, market trends, and economic indicators to forecast future property values. This allows investors to make more informed and strategic decisions, anticipating shifts in the market and positioning their portfolios for optimal returns. The predictive capabilities of AI not only reduce uncertainty but also empower investors to adapt to changing conditions with agility.

Machine learning, a subset of AI, plays a pivotal role in refining property valuation models. Traditional methods often rely on historical comparable, but machine learning algorithms can incorporate a broader array of variables, including neighborhood characteristics, economic indicators, and even sentiment analysis from social media. This holistic approach results in more accurate and dynamic property valuations, enhancing the precision of investment decisions.

Moreover, AI-driven data analytics facilitates risk assessment and mitigation in real estate investment. By analyzing historical data on property performance, market trends, and economic indicators, investors can identify potential risks and develop proactive strategies to mitigate them. Machine learning algorithms can continuously learn from new data, enabling real-time risk assessment and adaptive risk management strategies.

The concept of smart cities is gaining momentum, and AI contributes significantly to the realization of this vision. From optimizing traffic flow and energy consumption to enhancing public safety, AI applications in smart cities directly impact the desirability and value of real estate within these urban centers. Investors who understand and leverage these technological advancements position themselves strategically in markets at the forefront of innovation.

Customer experience and engagement are also elevated through AI applications in real estate. Chat bots and virtual assistants powered by AI enhance communication with potential buyers or tenants, providing instant information and assistance. This not only streamlines the transaction process but also improves customer satisfaction, contributing to positive relationships between investors and clients.

The democratization of real estate information is another notable contribution of AI. Access to comprehensive property data, market trends, and investment insights is no longer confined to experts. AI-driven platforms and tools empower individual investors with the information needed to make informed decisions, fostering a more inclusive and transparent real estate market.

Despite these advancements, it's crucial to acknowledge the ethical considerations associated with AI in real estate. Issues related to privacy, bias in algorithms, and the responsible use of data require careful consideration. The section encourages readers to approach AI with an ethical framework, ensuring that the benefits of technology are realized without compromising integrity and fairness.

In conclusion, "Unveiling the Power of Data Analytics in Real Estate" underscores the transformative influence of AI on the traditional paradigms of property investment. From predictive analytics and machine learning to risk assessment and smart city integration, AI is reshaping the way investors navigate the real estate market. As readers delve into this section, they gain insights into how harnessing the power of data analytics is not just an option but a strategic imperative in the pursuit of success in the dynamic world of real estate.

Section 2: Strategic Analysis and Timing

Navigating Market Cycles for Maximum Returns

In the intricate tapestry of real estate investing, understanding and navigating market cycles is a fundamental skill that separates astute investors from the rest. "Navigating Market Cycles for Maximum Returns," serves as a comprehensive guide for investors seeking to capitalize on the dynamic nature of real estate markets.

At its essence, a market cycle in real estate is characterized by phases of expansion, peak, contraction, and trough. Successful navigation through these cycles requires a nuanced understanding of the factors influencing each phase. The section begins by elucidating the signs and indicators that mark the different stages of a market cycle. Recognizing these cues empowers investors to make informed decisions about when to enter, hold, or exit the market.

During the expansion phase, characterized by rising property values and increased demand, investors are presented with opportunities for growth. The section explores strategies for maximizing returns during this period, emphasizing the importance of strategic acquisitions and leveraging properties for increased equity. It delves into the art of identifying emerging markets and property types poised for exponential growth, setting the stage for lucrative investments.

As the market approaches its peak, caution becomes paramount. The Section guides investors on how to recognize signs of saturation and overheating. Strategies for profit-taking and diversification are explored, allowing investors to capitalize on the appreciation achieved during the expansion phase. Understanding the inevitability of market cycles, the section encourages readers to adopt a disciplined approach, resisting the temptation to chase inflated values that may precede a contraction.

The contraction phase, often marked by declining property values and reduced demand, presents challenges but also opportunities for savvy investors. The section delves into strategies for navigating this downturn, such as identifying distressed properties, negotiating favorable deals, and positioning for future growth. It emphasizes the importance of liquidity during contractions, allowing investors to capitalize on distressed assets while maintaining financial flexibility.

Troughs in market cycles, representing the bottom of the downturn, offer unique opportunities for value investors. The Section also explores how to identify market bottoms and position for the eventual recovery. It discusses strategies such as strategic acquisitions, portfolio restructuring, and patient capital deployment. The section underscores the resilience and potential for substantial returns when investing during market troughs.

The concept of timing is a recurrent theme throughout the section, emphasizing the need for investors to align their strategies with the prevailing market conditions. It explores how economic indicators, interest rates, and external factors impact the timing of investment decisions. By adopting a proactive approach to market timing, investors position themselves to capitalize on opportunities and shield their portfolios from undue risks.

Risk management is another focal point in navigating market cycles. The section guides investors on how to assess and mitigate risks associated with each phase of the cycle. Diversification, liquidity management, and thorough due diligence emerge as key components of a robust risk mitigation strategy. Understanding that risk is inherent in real estate, the section equips readers with the tools to navigate uncertainties with resilience.

In conclusion, "Navigating Market Cycles for Maximum Returns" is not just a section; it's a strategic roadmap for investors aiming to extract the highest value from the undulating terrain of real estate markets. By comprehensively exploring the nuances of each market phase and providing actionable insights, this section empowers investors to navigate with confidence, make informed decisions, and ultimately achieve maximum returns in the ever-evolving world of real estate investing.

The Art of Timing: When to Buy and When to Sell

Timing is often cited as a critical factor in real estate success. "The Art of Timing: When to Buy and When to Sell," delves deeply into the intricate dance between market dynamics and strategic decision-making. This section serves as a masterclass for investors, providing insights into recognizing opportune moments to enter the market and judiciously exit for maximum returns.

The decision of when to buy is a nuanced process that begins with a thorough analysis of market indicators and trends. For instance, during a buyer's market—characterized by an oversupply of properties and reduced demand—investors can leverage their negotiating power to secure favorable deals. The section guides readers on how to identify such market conditions, examining factors like high inventory levels, longer days on market, and motivated sellers.

Conversely, recognizing the right time to buy may involve assessing economic indicators and demographic shifts that point to an upcoming surge in demand. For instance, a neighborhood undergoing revitalization, the construction of new infrastructure, or an influx of businesses can signal an opportune time to enter the market before property values rise.

Timing the sale of a property is equally crucial for optimizing returns. The section explores indicators that may suggest the market is reaching its peak, prompting investors to consider selling. For instance, rapidly rising property values, increased competition among buyers, and a decrease in the number of available properties may indicate that the market is approaching its zenith.

Strategic planning becomes paramount during a seller's market, where demand outpaces supply, leading to rising property values. The section delves into effective pricing strategies, staging techniques, and marketing approaches that can maximize a property's appeal and yield optimal returns. It also emphasizes the importance of aligning the sale with broader economic trends and interest rate movements.

Case studies serve as illustrative examples throughout the section, providing real-world scenarios of successful timing strategies. For instance, a savvy investor might have recognized the potential for growth in an up-and-coming neighborhood and strategically acquired properties before the area gained popularity. Similarly, another investor might have sold a property at its peak value just before a market correction, preserving gains and minimizing potential losses.

Market timing is not solely determined by external factors; it is also influenced by an investor's financial goals and risk tolerance. The section encourages readers to align their timing strategies with their investment objectives, whether focused on short-term gains, long-term appreciation, or a balanced portfolio approach.

Recognizing the cyclical nature of real estate markets, the section underscores the importance of patience and disciplined decision-making. It advises against impulsive actions driven by market hype or fear. Instead, investors are encouraged to adopt a strategic mindset, leveraging data analytics and market research to inform their timing decisions.

In conclusion, "The Art of Timing: When to Buy and When to Sell" is a section that demystifies the intricacies of market timing in real estate. By combining theoretical insights with practical examples, it equips investors with the knowledge and tools needed to navigate the delicate balance between seizing opportunities and protecting investments. As readers absorb the lessons within this section, they gain a profound understanding of the artistry involved in timing decisions—a skill that can significantly enhance their success in the ever-evolving world of real estate investing.

Creative Financing Strategies for High-Value Properties

In the pursuit of high-value properties, innovative and creative financing strategies become invaluable tools for investors seeking to maximize their financial leverage. Section 7, titled "Creative Financing Strategies for High-Value Properties," unfolds a tapestry of unconventional yet powerful approaches that go beyond traditional lending structures, opening doors to lucrative investment opportunities.

The section begins by exploring the concept of leverage, emphasizing how creative financing allows investors to amplify their purchasing power and undertake high-value acquisitions with a relatively smaller capital investment. One notable strategy is seller financing, where the property seller acts as the lender, offering flexible terms that can include lower down payments and customized repayment schedules.

Leveraging partnerships is another creative financing avenue discussed in the section. Collaborating with other investors, real estate professionals, or even private equity firms can provide access to additional capital and expertise. Joint ventures and equity partnerships enable investors to pool resources, mitigating financial risk and expanding the scope of their investment ventures.

The concept of creative financing extends to exploring alternative lending sources beyond traditional banks. The section explores the potential of private lenders, crowdfunding, and peer-to-peer lending platforms, each offering unique advantages such as faster approval processes, more flexible terms, and the ability to fund unconventional projects that may not align with conventional lending criteria.

Furthermore, the section delves into the strategic use of creative financing instruments such as wraparound mortgages, lease options, and subject-to financing. Each of these instruments offers distinct advantages, providing investors with the flexibility to structure deals that align with their financial goals and the unique attributes of high-value properties.

For instance, a wraparound mortgage involves creating a secondary mortgage that "wraps around" the existing one. This allows the investor to assume the seller's mortgage while creating a new, larger mortgage for the buyer. This strategy can be particularly effective in scenarios where interest rates are favorable, and the investor can profit from the spread between the existing mortgage rate and the new, higher-rate mortgage.

Lease options present an alternative avenue, allowing investors to control a high-value property without an immediate purchase. This strategy involves leasing the property with an option to buy at a predetermined price in the future. It provides the flexibility to secure a property with minimal upfront costs while potentially benefiting from appreciation over the lease term.

Subject-to financing involves acquiring a property "subject to" the existing financing already in place. This approach can be advantageous when dealing with favorable existing mortgage terms, enabling investors to take over the property with minimal initial investment and potentially capitalize on the existing financing structure.

Throughout the section, case studies and real-world examples illustrate the application of these creative financing strategies. These narratives provide insights into how investors have successfully structured deals, navigated challenges, and achieved high returns by thinking outside the traditional financing box.

In conclusion, "Creative Financing Strategies for High-Value Properties" is a section that invites investors to expand their toolkit and explore unconventional pathways in the pursuit of premium real estate. By embracing innovative financing approaches, investors can transcend financial barriers, unlock new opportunities, and position themselves strategically in the realm of high-value properties. As readers delve into the intricacies of this section, they gain a comprehensive understanding of the creative financing landscape—a landscape that holds the key to unlocking the full potential of high-value real estate investments.

Mastering Due Diligence: A Stress-Free Approach

In the intricate world of real estate investment, Section 8, titled "Mastering Due Diligence: A Stress-Free Approach," serves as a guiding beacon for investors navigating the complexities of property transactions. This section is a comprehensive exploration into the art and science of due diligence—an essential process that, when mastered, not only mitigates risks but also unveils opportunities, transforming the real estate investment landscape into a realm of informed decision-making.

The section commences with a foundational understanding of due diligence, emphasizing its role as the investigative process that precedes a property acquisition. It elucidates the multifaceted nature of due diligence, which involves comprehensive research, analysis, and verification of various aspects related to the property, market, and legal considerations. By establishing a solid conceptual framework, readers are prepared to approach due diligence as a strategic endeavor rather than a mere checklist.

A stress-free approach to due diligence is unveiled through systematic methodologies and organized frameworks. The section guides investors on developing due diligence checklists tailored to specific property types and investment goals. Such checklists serve as roadmaps, ensuring that no critical aspect is overlooked during the evaluation process. By breaking down the due diligence process into manageable steps, investors are equipped to conduct thorough investigations without succumbing to the overwhelm often associated with this critical stage.

Market analysis forms a pivotal component of due diligence, and the section explores how investors can delve into market trends, comparable sales, and future projections. By understanding the dynamics of the local real estate market, investors gain insights into property values, potential appreciation, and overall market health. The stress-free approach to market analysis involves leveraging data analytics, technology, and expert insights to paint a comprehensive picture of the property's market context.

Legal due diligence is an equally crucial aspect covered in the section. It delves into the meticulous examination of property titles, zoning regulations, easements, and potential legal encumbrances. By adopting a stress-free approach to legal scrutiny, investors learn how to collaborate with legal professionals, navigate complex documentation, and ensure that the property's legal standing aligns with their investment objectives. This meticulous examination serves as a safeguard against unforeseen legal challenges that could jeopardize the investment.

The section also explores the financial dimensions of due diligence, encompassing aspects such as property valuation, income analysis, and expense verification. Investors are guided on how to interpret financial statements, assess the property's income-generating potential, and identify opportunities for value enhancement. Through a stress-free financial due diligence approach, investors gain the confidence to make informed decisions grounded in a thorough understanding of the property's financial landscape.

Environmental due diligence emerges as another critical facet, addressing concerns related to potential environmental liabilities and regulatory compliance. The section provides insights into navigating environmental assessments, understanding the implications of environmental reports, and mitigating risks associated with contaminated properties. By adopting a proactive and stress-free approach to environmental due diligence, investors can safeguard their investments and contribute to sustainable practices.

Real-world case studies pepper the section, illustrating how mastering due diligence has been instrumental in the success of various real estate ventures. These examples showcase the application of due diligence principles in diverse scenarios, providing readers with practical insights into the challenges and triumphs encountered during the due diligence process.

In conclusion, "Mastering Due Diligence: A Stress-Free Approach" demystifies the intricate process of due diligence, offering investors a roadmap to navigate the complexities of property evaluation with confidence. By emphasizing a systematic and organized approach, the section empowers investors to conduct thorough due diligence without succumbing to stress, ensuring that their investment decisions are grounded in comprehensive research and strategic analysis. As readers absorb the wisdom embedded in this section, they embark on a journey towards mastery—an essential milestone in the pursuit of successful and stress-free real estate investing.

Section 3: Deal-Making and Negotiation

Negotiation Tactics for Securing the Best Deals

In the intricate dance of real estate transactions, "Negotiation Tactics for Securing the Best Deals," unravels the art and strategies behind successful negotiation. This section serves as a comprehensive guide for investors, shedding light on the nuanced tactics that can be employed to secure favorable terms, forge advantageous agreements, and ultimately, maximize returns in the highly competitive real estate market.

The section commences with an exploration of the fundamental principles that underpin effective negotiation in real estate. It emphasizes the importance of preparation, understanding the counterpart's motivations, and cultivating effective communication. Armed with these foundational principles, investors are better equipped to navigate the negotiation landscape with confidence.

One commonly used negotiation tactic explored in the section is the art of active listening. By actively listening to the counterpart's needs, concerns, and objectives, investors gain insights that can be leveraged strategically during negotiations. This tactic not only fosters rapport but also positions the negotiator to tailor proposals that address the specific interests of all parties involved, facilitating smoother and more successful transactions.

Understanding the concept of anchoring is another key aspect covered in the section. Anchoring involves presenting an initial offer or price point that serves as a reference point for the negotiation. Skilled negotiators can strategically set a favorable anchor, influencing subsequent discussions and potentially leading to more advantageous outcomes. The section delves into techniques for establishing strong anchors and leveraging them throughout the negotiation process.

Negotiating concessions is a common strategy explored in the section, wherein parties seek to secure favorable terms or additional benefits in exchange for concessions made in other areas. This can involve trade-offs in terms of price adjustments, property conditions, or closing timelines. By skillfully navigating the give-and-take of concessions, negotiators can create win-win scenarios that meet the needs of all parties involved.

The concept of creating urgency emerges as a potent negotiation tactic, especially in scenarios where timing plays a crucial role. The section delves into strategies for strategically introducing deadlines or time-sensitive elements into negotiations, compelling counterparties to make decisions promptly. This tactic can be particularly effective in competitive markets where securing a timely agreement is essential.

The section also explores the psychological aspects of negotiation, including the influence of non-verbal communication, body language, and emotional intelligence. Understanding how these factors impact the negotiation dynamic empowers investors to navigate conversations with heightened sensitivity, fostering positive interactions and building mutually beneficial relationships.

Negotiation tactics related to property information disclosure are discussed as well. Skilled negotiators know when and how to strategically reveal information about a property's condition, history, or market performance. The section provides insights into how controlled information disclosure can be used as a bargaining tool, influencing the negotiation process in favor of the investor.

Case studies and real-world examples pepper the section, illustrating how negotiation tactics have been applied successfully in diverse real estate scenarios. These examples serve as practical guides, showcasing how investors can adapt and implement various tactics based on the unique dynamics of each negotiation.

In conclusion, "Negotiation Tactics for Securing the Best Deals" is a section that elevates negotiation from a transactional process to an art form. By exploring a spectrum of tactics, investors gain a versatile toolkit that can be adapted to different situations, counterparties, and market conditions. As readers absorb the insights within this section, they embark on a journey towards mastering the delicate dance of negotiation—a skill set that is integral to achieving success and securing the best deals in the dynamic realm of real estate.

Leveraging Technology in Property Analysis

In the digital age, the convergence of real estate and technology has revolutionized the way investors analyze properties, providing a wealth of tools and data-driven insights. "Leveraging Technology in Property Analysis," serves as a beacon for investors seeking to harness the power of technological advancements to enhance their property evaluation processes and make more informed investment decisions.

The section commences by delving into the transformative role of data analytics in property analysis. Advanced algorithms and machine learning models can process vast datasets, offering investors actionable insights into market trends, property values, and investment potential. By understanding how to leverage these technologies, investors gain a competitive edge in identifying lucrative opportunities and mitigating risks through data-driven decision-making.

Geospatial technology takes center stage in the section, exploring how geographic information systems (GIS) and mapping tools contribute to property analysis. Investors can visualize property data overlaid with geographic features, enabling a comprehensive understanding of factors such as neighborhood demographics, amenities, and market trends. This spatial perspective enhances the precision of property evaluations and assists investors in selecting locations with the greatest growth potential.

The advent of virtual reality (VR) and augmented reality (AR) technologies has revolutionized property viewing and analysis. The section discusses how VR and AR applications allow investors to take virtual property tours, explore architectural designs, and envision potential renovations. These immersive experiences not only save time but also provide a more realistic understanding of a property's features and potential, facilitating more confident investment decisions.

Big data analytics in property analysis is explored as well, with an emphasis on how investors can leverage large datasets to identify patterns, correlations, and trends. This approach allows for more accurate property valuations, risk assessments, and market predictions. The section guides investors on how to access and interpret big data sources, transforming seemingly overwhelming information into actionable intelligence.

Block chain technology emerges as a disruptive force in property analysis, particularly in transactions and record-keeping. The section explains how block chain can streamline the property buying process by ensuring transparency, reducing fraud, and expediting transactions. By understanding the implications of block chain in real estate, investors can navigate a more efficient and secure property market.

Smart home technology is discussed within the context of property analysis, highlighting how Internet of Things (IoT) devices and home automation contribute to the evaluation of a property's efficiency, security, and market appeal. Investors can leverage insights from smart home technologies to assess a property's competitive positioning and potential for future value appreciation.

The section explores the utilization of predictive analytics in property analysis, allowing investors to forecast future market trends and property values. By understanding how predictive models are built and applying them to real estate scenarios, investors can make more informed decisions, whether in terms of timing the market, identifying growth opportunities, or adapting their investment strategies to changing conditions.

Real-world examples and case studies are integrated into the section, illustrating how technology-driven property analysis has been successfully applied in various investment scenarios. These examples showcase how investors can adapt and implement technological tools based on the unique attributes of each property and market.

In conclusion, "Leveraging Technology in Property Analysis" is a section that illuminates the path for investors to embrace and integrate technology into their property evaluation processes. By understanding the diverse applications of data analytics, geospatial technology, virtual reality, big data, block chain, and smart home technology, investors gain a holistic perspective on how to leverage technology to analyze properties with greater precision, efficiency, and insight. As readers delve into the insights within this section, they embark on a journey towards harnessing the full potential of technology in the dynamic and evolving landscape of real estate investing.

Section 4: Portfolio Building and Management

Building a Diverse Real Estate Portfolio

In the pursuit of sustainable and resilient real estate investments, "Building a Diverse Real Estate Portfolio," unfolds as a strategic guide for investors looking to construct a well-balanced and dynamic portfolio. Diversification, a cornerstone principle in investment strategy, takes center stage as the section navigates through various property types, geographic locations, and investment strategies to create a portfolio that withstands market fluctuations and maximizes long-term returns.

The section commences by elucidating the core concept of portfolio diversification in the context of real estate. Investors are guided to transcend the confines of a singular property type or location, recognizing that different assets exhibit distinct risk-return profiles. By diversifying across residential, commercial, industrial, and retail properties, investors can spread risk and capture diverse revenue streams, fostering stability and resilience in the face of market uncertainties.

Geographic diversification emerges as a critical component in building a robust real estate portfolio. The section explores how spreading investments across different markets, regions, and even countries can mitigate risks associated with localized economic downturns or market-specific challenges. Investors are encouraged to conduct thorough market research, assessing factors such as job growth, economic indicators, and demographic trends to strategically allocate assets across diverse geographies.

Property sector diversification is a focal point within the section, emphasizing the advantages of balancing assets across various real estate sectors. While residential properties may offer stability, commercial properties can provide higher rental yields. Industrial properties, on the other hand, may capitalize on the growing trend of ecommerce and logistics. By understanding the unique attributes of each sector, investors can optimize their portfolios for both income and appreciation.

Investment strategy diversification is explored as well, acknowledging that real estate offers various avenues for generating returns. From traditional buy-and-hold strategies to fix-and-flip approaches, as well as participation in real estate investment trusts (REITs) or crowdfunding platforms, the section guides investors on how to blend different strategies to achieve a well-rounded and adaptable portfolio.

Risk management is a recurrent theme throughout the section, underscoring the importance of aligning diversification with individual risk tolerance and investment goals. By carefully selecting assets with varying risk profiles, investors can strike a balance between stability and growth. The section encourages a strategic approach to risk, recognizing that calculated risks are inherent in real estate but can be managed through thoughtful diversification.

The section also explores the role of asset classes beyond physical properties, such as mortgage-backed securities and real estate-related stocks. Investors gain insights into how incorporating these financial instruments can add an additional layer of diversification to their real estate portfolios, enhancing liquidity and expanding investment opportunities beyond traditional ownership models.

Real-world case studies are seamlessly integrated into the section, showcasing how successful investors have applied diverse portfolio strategies to weather market downturns and capitalize on emerging opportunities. These examples serve as practical illustrations, demonstrating the tangible benefits of a well-considered and diversified real estate investment approach.

In conclusion, "Building a Diverse Real Estate Portfolio" is a section that invites investors to embrace the principles of diversification as a cornerstone of their real estate strategy. By navigating through the various dimensions of diversification—across property types, geographies, sectors, and investment strategies—investors can fortify their portfolios, creating a resilient and adaptable foundation for sustained success in the ever-evolving world of real estate investing. As readers absorb the insights within this section, they embark on a journey towards constructing portfolios that not only withstand market dynamics but thrive and grow amidst the complexities of the real estate landscape.

Risk Management and Mitigation in Real Estate Investing

In the dynamic realm of real estate investing, "Risk Management and Mitigation in Real Estate Investing," emerges as a strategic compass for investors seeking to navigate uncertainties and safeguard their investments. This section delves into the intricacies of risk, offering insights, methodologies, and practical approaches to identify, assess, and mitigate risks inherent in real estate ventures.

The section commences by establishing a foundational understanding of risk in the context of real estate. Investors are guided to recognize that risk is an inherent part of any investment, and effective risk management involves not only identifying potential threats but also implementing strategies to mitigate their impact. It emphasizes the proactive nature of risk management, encouraging investors to view it as a continuous and integral part of their investment journey.

Market risk, a prevalent factor in real estate, takes center stage in the section. Investors gain insights into how economic fluctuations, interest rate changes, and market downturns can impact property values and rental incomes. By conducting thorough market research and staying abreast of economic indicators, investors are equipped to anticipate and respond to market risks strategically, adjusting their investment strategies to align with prevailing market conditions.

Property-specific risks are explored in detail, ranging from physical property issues to title defects and environmental concerns. The section guides investors on how to conduct comprehensive due diligence to identify potential risks associated with a specific property. From engaging qualified inspectors to scrutinizing property documentation, thorough risk assessment forms the bedrock of effective risk mitigation strategies.

Financial risk, encompassing issues such as leverage and interest rate fluctuations, is a key focus within the section. Investors gain insights into the impact of financing choices on overall risk exposure and are guided on how to optimize their capital structure to manage financial risks effectively. The section explores scenarios where prudent financial management can mitigate risks associated with market volatility and interest rate fluctuations.

Legal and regulatory risks are examined, emphasizing the importance of staying informed about zoning regulations, building codes, and evolving legal landscapes. The section guides investors on how to collaborate with legal professionals to navigate complex legal considerations and ensure compliance with local laws. By adopting a proactive approach to legal risk management, investors can safeguard their investments against unforeseen legal challenges.

The section introduces the concept of risk mitigation strategies, exploring various tools and approaches to minimize the impact of identified risks. These strategies include diversification, insurance, contingency planning, and incorporating risk factors into investment decision-making. By understanding and implementing these risk mitigation techniques, investors can enhance the resilience of their real estate portfolios.

Scenario analysis and stress testing emerge as valuable tools in risk management, allowing investors to assess the potential impact of adverse events on their investments. The section provides guidance on how to conduct scenario analyses, enabling investors to model different market conditions and prepare contingency plans to navigate potential challenges.

Real-world case studies are seamlessly integrated into the section, illustrating how successful investors have navigated and mitigated risks in diverse real estate scenarios. These examples serve as practical demonstrations of effective risk management strategies, showcasing the importance of foresight and adaptability in the face of uncertainties.

In conclusion, "Risk Management and Mitigation in Real Estate Investing" is a section that empowers investors to embrace risk as an integral part of their investment journey while providing the tools and strategies to manage and mitigate potential challenges. By adopting a proactive and informed approach to risk, investors can enhance the resilience of their real estate portfolios, fostering sustained success in an ever-evolving market. As readers absorb the insights within this section, they embark on a journey towards mastering the delicate balance between risk-taking and risk management—a skill set essential for navigating the complexities of real estate investing.

Section 5: Psychological and Interpersonal Aspects

The Psychology of Successful Real Estate Investment

In the intricate world of real estate investing, "The Psychology of Successful Real Estate Investment," delves into the profound impact of human behavior, emotions, and cognitive biases on investment decisions. This section serves as a psychological compass for investors, unraveling the intricacies of the human mind in the context of real estate transactions and providing insights into how mastering the psychological aspects of investing can lead to more successful and informed decision-making.

The section begins by exploring the psychological factors that influence investor behavior, acknowledging the role of emotions such as fear, greed, and overconfidence in shaping decision-making processes. Investors gain an understanding of how these emotions can lead to impulsive actions, herd behavior, or the avoidance of calculated risks, impacting the overall success of their real estate ventures.

Emotional intelligence takes center stage as the section delves into the importance of self-awareness and self-regulation in the investment process. Successful investors learn to recognize their own emotional triggers and biases, allowing them to make decisions rooted in rationality rather than being swayed by transient feelings. By fostering emotional intelligence, investors can navigate the peaks and valleys of the real estate market with resilience and composure.

Behavioral finance principles are seamlessly integrated into the section, shedding light on cognitive biases that can cloud judgment and hinder sound decision-making. Investors are guided through an exploration of biases such as anchoring, confirmation bias, and loss aversion, learning how to identify and counteract these mental pitfalls in the context of real estate investments. Awareness of these biases empowers investors to approach decisions with a clearer and more objective mindset.

The section also delves into the psychological aspects of risk tolerance and risk perception. Investors gain insights into how individual differences in risk appetite and the framing of risk can impact decision-making. Understanding one's risk tolerance and adopting strategies to align it with investment goals is presented as a key psychological element in building a successful real estate portfolio.

The concept of mental accounting is explored within the context of real estate investment, emphasizing how investors categorize and perceive different types of investments. By understanding how mental accounting influences decision-making, investors can optimize their portfolios and allocate resources strategically, ensuring a more holistic and purposeful approach to real estate investments.

The section introduces the role of overconfidence in real estate investing, examining how an inflated sense of one's own abilities and knowledge can lead to suboptimal decisions. Investors are guided on how to cultivate humility and openness to feedback, fostering a mindset that encourages continuous learning and adaptation in the face of changing market conditions.

Real-world examples and case studies are seamlessly integrated into the section, illustrating how successful investors have navigated psychological challenges to achieve their real estate goals. These examples serve as practical illustrations of the psychological principles discussed, showcasing how a nuanced understanding of the human mind can lead to more effective decision-making and ultimately, success in real estate investing.

In conclusion, "The Psychology of Successful Real Estate Investment" is a section that invites investors to delve into the depths of human behavior and cognition to unlock the secrets of successful real estate investing. By understanding and mastering the psychological aspects of decision-making, investors can cultivate resilience, enhance emotional intelligence, and navigate the complexities of the real estate market with a strategic and informed mindset. As readers absorb the insights within this section, they embark on a journey towards not only understanding the psychology of successful real estate investment but leveraging it as a powerful tool in their investment journey.

Building Relationships for Insider Insights

In the dynamic world of real estate, success is not solely measured by market knowledge or financial acumen; it's also about the art of building meaningful relationships. This principle forms the cornerstone of our comprehensive guide, "Smart Real Estate Insights: Navigating Success Through Relationships and Strategy." This book transcends traditional investment advice, offering a holistic approach that intertwines the importance of cultivating genuine connections with strategic insights into the real estate market.

At the heart of this guide is the section titled "Building Relationships for Insider Insights." In an industry where information is power, this section unravels the significance of establishing and nurturing relationships with key players in the real estate ecosystem. From seasoned real estate agents and property developers to local community leaders, each connection holds the potential to unlock invaluable insights and opportunities. We delve into the art of networking, providing practical tips on how to build relationships authentically and leverage them for exclusive market intelligence.

The book doesn't stop at the interpersonal dynamics of real estate; it extends its reach into the realms of strategic investing. Sections such as "The Fundamentals of Smart Investing in Real Estate" and "Leveraging Technology in Property Analysis" equip readers with the essential knowledge to make informed decisions. Whether you're a novice investor seeking guidance on market trends or a seasoned pro looking to harness the power of data analytics and technology, this guide offers a roadmap for success.

Navigating market cycles, mastering due diligence, and understanding the psychology of successful real estate investment are among the other sections that provide readers with a comprehensive toolkit. Real-world case studies pepper the pages, offering tangible examples of investors who have successfully applied the principles outlined in the book to achieve their real estate goals.

"Smart Real Estate Insights" is not just a guide; it's a mentor that empowers readers to navigate the intricacies of real estate with confidence. By emphasizing the symbiotic relationship between relationship-building and strategic investing, this book transcends conventional wisdom, inviting readers to embark on a journey where insider insights, coupled with sound strategy, become the keys to unlocking lasting success in the ever-evolving landscape of real estate investing

Section 6: Exit Strategies and Future Planning

Exit Strategies for Optimal Returns

In the intricate dance of real estate investing, the ability to navigate exit strategies with finesse is often the hallmark of a successful investor. This Section of our comprehensive guide, serves as a strategic compass for investors looking to optimize their returns and ensure a smooth transition from property ownership. This section unravels a spectrum of exit strategies, offering insights into how each approach can be tailored to specific investment goals and market conditions.

The section commences with an exploration of the traditional exit strategy of selling a property for a profit. Investors gain insights into market timing, pricing strategies, and effective marketing techniques to maximize returns during a sale. Whether in a seller's market or a buyer's market, the section guides investors on how to strategically position their properties for optimal outcomes, considering factors such as property condition, local market dynamics, and broader economic trends.

The concept of refinancing as an exit strategy is dissected within the section. Investors learn how to leverage increased property values or improved financial profiles to secure favorable refinancing terms. This approach allows investors to extract equity from a property while retaining ownership, providing liquidity for other investments or property improvements.

The section explores the realm of 1031 exchanges, a tax-deferred strategy that enables investors to sell a property and reinvest the proceeds into a like-kind property. By understanding the intricacies of 1031 exchanges, investors can defer capital gains taxes, allowing for the continuous growth of their real estate portfolios. The section provides practical guidance on navigating the regulatory requirements and timelines associated with this strategic exit approach.

The concept of holding for long-term cash flow emerges as another exit strategy explored in the section. Investors gain insights into the benefits of building a portfolio of income-generating properties that provide a steady stream of cash flow over an extended period. This strategy is particularly suitable for investors with a focus on passive income and long-term wealth accumulation.

The section introduces the concept of selling partial interests or fractionalizing ownership as a unique exit strategy. By selling a percentage of ownership to other investors, property owners can unlock liquidity without relinquishing full control. This approach is examined in the context of crowdfunding platforms and real estate investment trusts (REITs), providing investors with alternative avenues to exit their investments while diversifying risk.

Real-world case studies are seamlessly integrated into the section, illustrating how successful investors have strategically employed various exit strategies to optimize returns based on their specific circumstances and objectives. These examples serve as practical guides, showcasing the versatility and adaptability required in the ever-evolving landscape of real estate investing.

In conclusion, "Exit Strategies for Optimal Returns" is a section that equips investors with the knowledge and tools to navigate the culmination of their real estate ventures strategically. By unraveling a spectrum of exit strategies and providing insights into their application, this section empowers investors to make informed decisions that align with their financial goals and market conditions. As readers absorb the insights within this section, they embark on a journey towards mastering the art of exits—a skill set essential for maximizing returns and ensuring sustained success in the dynamic world of real estate investing.

Case Studies: Learning from Profitable Investments

In the realm of real estate, the ability to glean insights from successful investments is a powerful tool for aspiring investors. Let's explore two real case studies that provide valuable lessons and highlight key strategies employed by individuals who have navigated the intricacies of real estate, reaping substantial profits in the process.

Case Study 1: Strategic Renovation and Appreciation

In this case study, we examine the journey of Jane, an astute investor who identified a distressed property in an up-and-coming neighborhood. Recognizing the potential for appreciation, Jane negotiated a favorable purchase price and embarked on a strategic renovation project. The key takeaways from Jane's success include:

- **Meticulous Due Diligence:** Jane thoroughly researched the property, assessing its condition, market dynamics, and potential for improvement. This diligence allowed her to make informed decisions and accurately estimate the costs involved in the renovation.

- **Creative Financing:** To fund the acquisition and renovation, Jane explored creative financing options. Leveraging a mix of traditional loans, private financing, and personal resources, she structured a financial package that maximized her return on investment.

- **Strategic Renovation:** Instead of merely addressing cosmetic issues, Jane strategically renovated the property to align with the preferences of the target market. This thoughtful approach not only enhanced the property's aesthetic appeal but also increased its overall market value.

- **Timing the Market:** Jane timed her investment well, capitalizing on the neighborhood's upward trajectory. As the area experienced increased demand, the renovated property appreciated significantly, allowing Jane to sell at a substantial profit.

Case Study 2: Long-Term Buy-and-Hold Success

In this case study, we explore the journey of John, an investor with a focus on long-term wealth accumulation through a buy-and-hold strategy. John's success lies in his ability to build and manage a resilient portfolio of income-generating properties. Key lessons from John's strategy include:

- **Strategic Location Selection:** John prioritized properties in areas with strong rental demand, favorable economic indicators, and potential for long-term growth. This strategic location selection laid the foundation for sustained cash flow.

- **Tenant Management:** John implemented effective tenant management practices, fostering positive landlord-tenant relationships. This approach not only minimized vacancy rates but also contributed to a stable and consistent stream of rental income.

- **Adaptive Portfolio Management:** Recognizing the evolving nature of real estate markets, John embraced an adaptive approach to portfolio management. He periodically assessed market trends, adjusted rental rates, and made strategic acquisitions to optimize the performance of his portfolio.

- **Financial Resilience:** John prioritized financial resilience by maintaining adequate cash reserves for unforeseen expenses, market downturns, or opportunities for strategic acquisitions. This approach allowed him to weather economic fluctuations and capitalize on favorable market conditions.

These case studies exemplify the diversity of successful real estate strategies, emphasizing the importance of strategic planning, market awareness, and adaptability. By learning from the experiences of investors like Jane and John, aspiring real estate enthusiasts can gain valuable insights to inform their own investment decisions and increase the likelihood of success in the dynamic world of real estate.

Future-Proofing Your Real Estate Investments

As the landscape of real estate continues to evolve, the imperative to future-proof investments has become paramount. This section of our comprehensive guide, titled "Future-Proofing Your Real Estate Investments," serves as a strategic compass for investors seeking to not only navigate the present but also anticipate and prepare for the challenges and opportunities of the future.

The section commences by examining the impact of technological advancements on the real estate industry. From the integration of artificial intelligence in property analysis to the rise of smart home technologies, investors are guided on how to leverage these innovations to enhance property value, tenant experience, and overall investment performance.

Climate resilience takes center stage as the section explores strategies to future-proof properties against the impacts of climate change. Investors gain insights into sustainable building practices, energy-efficient upgrades, and the incorporation of eco-friendly features that not only align with environmental consciousness but also contribute to long-term cost savings and property value appreciation.

The concept of adaptive reuse is dissected within the section, offering investors a lens into how underutilized or obsolete properties can be transformed to meet changing market demands. Case studies illustrate successful adaptive reuse projects, showcasing the versatility of real estate investments in adapting to evolving societal needs.

A thorough exploration of demographic shifts and lifestyle trends provides investors with the tools to anticipate future demand. From the rise of remote work influencing housing preferences to the increasing demand for urban amenities in suburban areas, the section delves into how understanding demographic shifts can inform strategic investment decisions.

The integration of ESG (Environmental, Social, and Governance) principles into real estate investments is examined. Investors are guided on how adopting socially responsible and sustainable practices not only aligns with ethical considerations but also enhances the resilience and attractiveness of their investment portfolios in a world increasingly focused on environmental and social responsibility.

The section also explores the concept of "future-proof neighborhoods," emphasizing the importance of investing in areas with robust infrastructure, connectivity, and amenities that are likely to remain attractive to future generations. Readers gain insights into how foresight in neighborhood selection contributes to long-term investment success.

Real-world examples and case studies are seamlessly integrated into the section, illustrating how successful investors have future-proofed their real estate portfolios. These examples serve as practical demonstrations of the strategies discussed, showcasing how a forward-thinking approach can contribute to sustained success in an ever-changing real estate landscape.

In conclusion, "Future-Proofing Your Real Estate Investments" is a section that equips investors with the knowledge and tools to anticipate and adapt to the future of real estate. By embracing technological innovations, sustainable practices, and a strategic understanding of demographic and societal shifts, investors can position themselves not only to weather future challenges but also to thrive and capitalize on emerging opportunities. As readers absorb the insights within this section, they embark on a journey towards future-proofing their real estate investments—a proactive and strategic approach essential for long-term success in the dynamic world of real estate investing.

Section 7: Passive Income and Property Enhancement

Passive Income Streams in Real Estate

In the pursuit of financial freedom and flexibility, the concept of passive income streams in real estate has emerged as a beacon for investors seeking to generate revenue with minimal ongoing effort. This section is a roadmap for investors looking to cultivate a portfolio that not only appreciates in value but also provides a steady and hands-off stream of income.

The section commences by exploring the fundamentals of passive income in real estate, emphasizing the distinction between active and passive investment strategies. Investors gain insights into how strategic property selection, efficient property management, and leveraging technology contribute to the creation of income-generating assets that require minimal day-to-day involvement.

One of the primary avenues for passive income in real estate—rental properties—is dissected within the section. Readers gain practical guidance on how to select properties with strong rental potential, screen tenants effectively, and implement streamlined property management processes. The goal is to create a source of consistent cash flow that requires minimal direct involvement from the investor.

The section also explores the concept of real estate investment trusts (REITs) as a vehicle for passive income. Investors learn about the benefits of investing in REITs, which provide an opportunity to participate in real estate markets without the hands-on responsibilities of property ownership. The section provides insights into how to evaluate and select REITs that align with individual investment goals.

Passive income through real estate crowdfunding platforms is another avenue explored within the section. By participating in crowdfunding projects, investors can diversify their portfolios without the need for active property management. The section guides readers on how to navigate crowdfunding platforms, assess potential projects, and manage the associated risks.

The integration of short-term rentals, such as vacation properties or Airbnb listings, into a passive income strategy is examined. Investors gain insights into the considerations for successful short-term rental investments, including property location, market demand, and effective marketing strategies to maximize occupancy rates.

The concept of seller financing is explored as a means to create passive income streams through seller-backed mortgages. Investors learn how to structure seller financing deals, negotiate favorable terms, and create a source of ongoing income through interest payments.

Tax efficiency in passive income strategies is a recurring theme within the section. Investors are guided on how to leverage tax advantages associated with passive real estate investments, including depreciation deductions, 1031 exchanges, and other tax incentives that can enhance overall returns.

Real-world case studies are seamlessly integrated into the section, illustrating how successful investors have cultivated passive income streams in diverse real estate scenarios. These examples serve as practical demonstrations of the strategies discussed, showcasing how a well-designed passive income strategy can contribute to financial stability and freedom.

In conclusion, "Passive Income Streams in Real Estate" is a section that empowers investors to not only build wealth through property appreciation but also cultivate streams of income that require minimal ongoing effort. By understanding and implementing passive income strategies such as rental properties, REITs, crowdfunding, short-term rentals, and seller financing, investors can create a diversified and resilient portfolio that aligns with their financial goals while providing the freedom to enjoy life beyond active property management. As readers absorb the insights within this section, they embark on a journey towards unlocking the full potential of passive income streams in the dynamic and rewarding world of real estate investing.

The Art of Adding Value to Your Properties

In the dynamic realm of real estate, the strategic enhancement of a property's value is an art form that savvy investors master to maximize returns and create a competitive edge in the market. "The Art of Adding Value to Your Properties," delves into the nuanced strategies and creative approaches that can transform a property into a lucrative asset.

The section commences by emphasizing the importance of thorough market research and understanding local trends. Successful investors grasp the intricacies of the target market, identifying the demands and preferences of potential buyers or tenants. This insight guides the selection of value-adding improvements that resonate with the specific needs of the demographic, ensuring a targeted and impactful enhancement.

Renovation and modernization emerge as key components of the value-adding process. Investors gain insights into identifying areas of improvement, whether through cosmetic enhancements, structural upgrades, or the integration of modern amenities. The section provides guidance on conducting cost-effective renovations that yield a substantial increase in property value, striking a balance between investment and return.

Strategic landscaping is explored as a subtle yet influential tool in adding value to properties. From enhancing curb appeal to creating functional outdoor spaces, landscaping contributes not only to aesthetics but also to the overall perceived value of a property. Readers learn how thoughtful landscaping choices can attract potential buyers or tenants and elevate the desirability of a property.

The section also delves into the concept of energy-efficient upgrades as a means to add value. In an era where sustainability is increasingly prioritized, investors gain insights into cost-effective measures such as energy-efficient appliances, insulation improvements, and smart home technologies. These enhancements not only appeal to environmentally conscious individuals but also contribute to long-term cost savings, adding tangible value to the property.

Creative floor plan optimization is another dimension explored within the section. Investors learn how to identify underutilized spaces and reconfigure layouts to maximize functionality and appeal. This strategic approach not only enhances the living experience for occupants but also positions the property as a valuable and adaptable asset in the market.

The integration of technology emerges as a contemporary avenue for adding value. Investors gain insights into leveraging smart home features, security systems, and energy management solutions to enhance the property's appeal. The section guides readers on how to stay abreast of technological advancements that align with market demands and contribute to the overall value proposition of the property.

Real-world case studies seamlessly woven into the section illustrate how successful investors have applied these value-adding principles to their properties. These examples serve as practical demonstrations of the artistry involved in strategically enhancing property value, showcasing the transformative impact of thoughtful and well-executed improvements.

In conclusion, "The Art of Adding Value to Your Properties" is a section that invites investors to elevate their approach to property ownership beyond the transactional. By embracing the art of adding value, investors not only enhance the financial returns of their investments but also contribute to the overall vibrancy and sustainability of the real estate market. As readers absorb the insights within this section, they embark on a journey towards mastering the delicate balance between investment and enhancement—a skill set essential for success in the ever-evolving world of real estate investing.

Section 8: Culmination and Recap

The Road to Stress-Free, High-Return Real Estate Investing

Embarking on the road to stress-free, high-return real estate investing is the culmination of strategic planning, informed decision-making, and a holistic approach to property management. Section 20 of our comprehensive guide serves as a navigational beacon, guiding investors toward a path where financial success aligns harmoniously with peace of mind.

The section opens by emphasizing the importance of setting clear investment goals and cultivating a realistic mindset. Investors are encouraged to define their financial objectives, risk tolerance, and preferred level of involvement in property management. This foundational step sets the tone for a stress-free journey, aligning expectations with the realities of the real estate market.

Effective due diligence emerges as a cornerstone of stress-free investing. The section provides a comprehensive guide on how to conduct thorough research, from evaluating market trends and property values to assessing potential risks. By equipping investors with the tools to make informed decisions, due diligence becomes a proactive strategy for mitigating uncertainties and minimizing stress.

Strategic property selection is explored as a means to optimize returns while minimizing potential headaches. Investors gain insights into identifying properties with strong growth potential, attractive rental yields, and manageable maintenance requirements. The section guides readers on how to align property choices with their investment goals, fostering a portfolio that is both lucrative and low-stress.

The integration of professional assistance is a key theme within the section. Whether engaging with experienced real estate agents, property managers, or legal professionals, investors learn how to build a support network that alleviates the burdens of day-to-day management. This collaborative approach allows investors to leverage the expertise of professionals and focus on the aspects of real estate that align with their strengths and preferences.

Risk management and contingency planning emerge as essential components of stress-free investing. The section provides insights into anticipating potential challenges, from market fluctuations to unexpected property issues. By adopting a proactive stance and having contingency plans in place, investors are better prepared to navigate uncertainties with composure.

The section also explores the concept of leveraging technology for streamlined property management. From digital tools for market analysis to smart home technologies for remote monitoring, investors gain insights into how embracing technological advancements can enhance efficiency and reduce the stress associated with property ownership.

Real-world case studies are seamlessly integrated into the section, illustrating how successful investors have applied these stress-free strategies to their real estate portfolios. These examples serve as practical demonstrations of how a deliberate and strategic approach can lead to high returns while maintaining a sense of tranquility in the investment journey.

In conclusion, "The Road to Stress-Free, High-Return Real Estate Investing" is a section that encapsulates the essence of a balanced and purposeful approach to real estate investment. By emphasizing clarity in goals, diligent research, strategic decision-making, and leveraging professional support, investors can traverse the road to financial success with a sense of confidence and tranquility. As readers absorb the insights within this section, they embark on a journey towards achieving high returns without compromising peace of mind—an equilibrium that defines the pinnacle of real estate investing success.

Closing

As we arrive at the closing section of "Smart Real Estate Investing: Discover Lucrative Properties Stress-Free for High Returns," it's not merely the end of a book—it marks the beginning of your empowered journey in the world of real estate. Throughout this comprehensive guide, we've navigated the intricacies of smart investing, from understanding market fundamentals to leveraging technology, and from cultivating passive income to future-proofing your investments.

As you reflect on the diverse sections that have unfolded, each revealing a piece of the intricate puzzle that is real estate investing, remember that this isn't just a manual but a blueprint for your success. You've explored the art of adding value to properties, learned from real case studies, and uncovered the psychology behind successful investments. Now, armed with knowledge, strategy, and foresight, you stand on the threshold of a world of possibilities.

Your journey is not just about financial gains; it's about creating a stress-free, high-return portfolio that aligns with your aspirations and values. Whether you're a seasoned investor seeking to refine your strategies or a newcomer venturing into the exciting realm of real estate, this guide has been crafted to empower you at every step.

Remember, real estate is not just about buildings and transactions—it's about relationships, creativity, and adaptability. It's about anticipating trends, understanding the psychology of the market, and strategically adding value to your properties. It's a journey that requires not just financial acumen but also a touch of artistry—an art of turning properties into thriving assets.

As you venture into the diverse landscapes of real estate, embrace the challenges as opportunities and the setbacks as lessons. Build relationships, leverage technology, and always keep an eye on the ever-evolving future of the market. Your success lies not just in the numbers on a balance sheet but in the stories of properties transformed, challenges overcome, and goals realized.

So, as you turn the last page of this guide, remember that you hold the keys to unlock the doors of your real estate success. Whether it's the thrill of a strategic acquisition, the satisfaction of adding value to a property, or the joy of cultivating a passive income stream, your journey is a tapestry woven with each decision, each insight, and each strategic move.

May your real estate endeavors be marked by prosperity, resilience, and the fulfillment of your financial goals. As you step into the world of smart real estate investing, may you discover not only lucrative properties but also the fulfillment that comes from navigating this dynamic landscape with wisdom and purpose.

Here's to your success, your journey, and the countless possibilities that await you in the captivating world of real estate. Happy investing!